A LINE IN THE WATER

A LINE IN THE WATER

H. RICK GOFF

*Fishing shared with Fishing Buddies,
Friendship, Faith & Family*

Edited by: Lillie Ammann
Layout by: Jan McClintock

ISBN: 978-1-7324195-0-6

CDF
CEDRIC D. FISHER & COMPANY
PUBLISHERS

DEDICATION

This book is dedicated to all my fishing buddies who share my passion for having "A Line in The Water!"

TABLE OF CONTENTS

FOREWORD

by Kathy Batts

A Line in the Water is a pure enjoyment to read. Rick invites us along to share his nostalgic journey reflecting upon his many fishing adventures. It's a journey filled with adventure, passion, and most of all the bonds of friendship. I'm not a fisherman, but quickly realized the stories were about more than fishing.

Being an Officer in the United States Air Force, Rick was fortunate to have had many opportunities for extensive travel as well as many moves. This provided a variety of fishing adventures in countless locations. With a handshake, a stranger became a new fishing buddy for Rick.

My husband, Bill Batts, was one of those fortunate fishing buddies. Rick and his family became our new neighbors when one of his moves brought them to Tampa, Florida. Rick and my husband developed a friendship and formed a special bond centered around their love of fishing. I was so happy my husband found a new fishing buddy! Now he could share his love for the sport with someone who understood the joys, adventures, tranquility, and most of all the bond that is made during a great fishing trip.

As Rick shares in the book, "part of the beauty of life is having different experiences and making the most of them."

Rick is one of those special people that when you meet him, you immediately feel his passion and compassion for life and for the people he meets along the way. Rick's accounts of his fishing adventures reflect his enthusiasm for life and the importance of friendship, growth, and passion. I am so thankful Rick was a part of our lives. He gave my husband Bill many wonderful fishing experiences which brought him much peace and tranquility near the end of his life. Rick was there for him and provided him prayers and peace during his final fishing trip. One could not ask for a better fishing buddy than Rick was to Bill.

As a reader of *A Line in The Water*, you will feel the sincerity with which Rick tells his stories. He writes from the heart and this wonderful read will bring you much laughter, adventure, and even a few tears. I now recognize the importance of appreciating the moments in one's life while doing the things you are passionate about. Rick has accomplished many great things and this book is one of them.

INTRODUCTION

From childhood to adulthood, fishing evolved from a hobby into a passion. It has been one of the constants in my life, always there. While on active duty in the Air Force, one of the top priorities during my many moves was to find my next favorite fishing hole—the place I knew I would need to allow me to escape and recalibrate. While I worked as a business executive, one of the top priorities once I relocated was to find my next favorite fishing hole. Again, this would be the place I knew I would need to allow me to escape and recalibrate.

I love to fish. I don't mean fishing in bass tournaments, wearing fancy fishing gear patches on my shirt, and owning a fast fishing boat. I don't mean fishing for a living, like commercial fishermen. I mean the simple pleasure of having a line in the water while waiting for the next bite, after making the perfect cast, in the perfect spot.

Fishing has been a common bond that linked me to perfect strangers who would become *fishing buddies*. Some became lifelong friends, while others were great friends for only a season in my life. But we all shared a common passion for fishing.

A Line in the Water is not about how to fish. It is about the four F's in my life: faith, family, friends, and fishing.

The following chapters highlight my love for my childhood hobby and the way it added a completeness to my life. They also share fishing adventures with fishing buddies who were former bosses, mentors, perfect strangers, and family. The vignettes of the book occurred over my lifetime, but to me, they all seem like they happened just yesterday.

CHAPTER 1: FISHING BUDDY QUOTES

The following are funny and serious quotes and observations made by me and my fishing buddies while we had a line in the water:

"Fish on."

"That water looks cold."

"I can catch fish in a mudhole."

"Who is going to clean all these fish?"

"What is catch and release?"

"That fish is too small to keep."

"What do you mean this fish is too small to keep? It's the biggest fish I ever caught!"

"The fish broke my line."

"The rod and reel went straight into the water and never stopped going."

"How are we going to get him out of the water?"

"I'm not touching that thing."

"Cut the line—it's a shark."

"Look at it like this; since we got skunked, we don't have to worry about cleaning any fish tonight."

"We might have to stop and buy some fish. How else are our wives going to believe we were out fishing all day and didn't catch anything?"

"I don't need a boat. I just need a friend who has a boat."

"Feels like a big one."

"The bait's bigger than that fish."

"Is that the fish or the bait?"

"Did you get the bait?"

"That's the bait! What are we trying to catch?"

"Ouch—it's got sharp teeth."

"Dad, did I do good at fishing?"

"I think the boat is out of gas."

"Were those the car keys that just fell in the water?"

"Was that a shark that just swam by us?"

"SNAKE!!!!"

"Do you know how to throw that casting net?"

"What a beautiful sunrise."

"What a gorgeous sunset."

"How do you take the fish off the hook without hurting them?"

"Did you take the Dramamine I gave you?"

"I think I'm going to be sick."

"How early do you think we need to leave?" "O dark-thirty."

"These mosquitoes are terrible."

"The fish is dragging the boat!"

"Something just bumped my leg."

"That's why it's called fishing and not catching."

"I think the tide is coming in—the water is at my chest. We had better get in the canoe."

"Did you tie off the canoe?"

"Just try to keep your eyes on the shoreline."

"These waves are too high."

"I can't even think about holding a rod right now. I might fall overboard."

"What a great way to end the day—catching a fish with the last bait with my favorite fishing buddy."

CHAPTER 2: FISHING VS. CATCHING

One big misconception about fishing is the premise that you have to catch fish to enjoy the experience of fishing. I know it sounds counter-intuitive, but catching fish is just the bonus of fishing and only part of the overall experience.

I enjoy the simple act of casting and reeling in my bait. I even appreciate the small waves made by the fishing line as it glides through the water. Of course, I love to catch a nice bass or whatever I might be fishing for at the time. But, if I don't, I'm still content, because I have my rod in my hands, and I get to live in the moment while I am fishing.

Fishermen know exactly what I'm talking about. They get it and understand that the anticipation of waiting for the next bite is just as much a part of fishing as hooking and reeling in the big one.

Over the years, I have enjoyed some of the best times on fishing trips. Taking in a beautiful sunrise or a sunset with a fishing buddy, sharing life experiences, is the best. Talking about fishing and hearing fish stories about "the big one that got away" is a good time in and of itself.

I also enjoy being alone, living in the moment, while I have a line in the water. I appreciate how fishing slows down the pace of my life and allows me to almost feel my next breath.

In my day, I have missed catching a few big fish. I thought I had them well hooked, watched them jump out of the water, and usually reeled them within two feet of me. Then, at the last second, the fish would spit the hook out and swim away. I don't get upset, because that's the nature of fishing. Sometimes you catch them, and sometimes they shake the hook and swim away. I simply keep fishing and keep my line in the water.

CHAPTER 3: THE CREEK

Columbus, Georgia

Bull Creek was my first favorite fishing hole. The Creek (as we called it) was a part of the neighborhood where I grew up in Columbus, Georgia. It had all the trappings that would keep young adventurous boys occupied. There were raging rapids in some areas, slow moving stream in others, and, of course, a nice fishing hole full of bass, catfish, brim, carp, and unknown species of fish, at least unknown to us.

My friends and I spent countless hours down at the creek exploring the forest along the banks, looking for turtles and avoiding snakes, but we mostly fished. It was our summer hangout; I can remember summers growing up when I think I fished at the creek every day! During the hot and humid Georgia summer days, there was nothing like hanging out in a shady spot on the creek swimming or just watching the water flow by.

Some adults would even go to the creek and fish, but it was mostly a kids' hangout. My mom was not a big fan of the creek, but she knew I loved to fish and didn't mind that I spent so much time there.

I was in the seventh grade and had learned to play the upright bass in school. The thing was almost three times my size, but I did eventually get it figured out. We had been practicing for our big concert all year, and it was time for us to give our big performance for our parents at the end of the school term. We were going to wow our parents with a middle school version of some of the songs from the musical *Fiddler on the Roof.* I absolutely loved those songs and still hum them today.

School was out at 2:30, and I was home by 3:30. I felt I had time to go down to the creek and get in a couple of hours of fishing before I had to go to my concert that evening. That's how the mind of twelve-year old boys work; they think they have time to do everything or at least the things they want to do. Thus, I felt I had time to get to the creek, catch a few fish, and get back home before we had to leave for my big concert.

I had been fishing for about an hour when I hooked the biggest bass I had ever seen in the creek. I had a worm on a bobber in one of the deeper holes of the creek when suddenly my little Zepco rod almost flew out of my hands. The fish pulled so hard that I thought the line was going to snap, but fortunately I had the drag set and the fish just took line until I could gather myself and set the hook. My heart was pumping with excitement as the bass jumped out of the water trying to spit the hook out. But he was hooked well, and I slowly started to reel him in. All I could think of was that I couldn't wait to tell my friends about the big fish I had caught.

That's when I heard my brother Bo calling me. He had run to the creek, and he had an anxious sound in his voice like someone was in trouble—and I sensed that someone was me.

I continued to reel the bass in, and between the breaths of excitement, it hit me: I had forgotten all about my big concert that evening. While almost out of breath, Bo told me we were late, and Mom was waiting for me to come home and get dressed so we could go to the school for my concert. He gave me that look of doom, like this may not only be your last day fishing at the creek, but it may be your last day on earth. He said Mom was really mad, and I had better be prepared for the worst. Bo and I normally teased each other and exaggerated about stuff like this, but this time I knew he was serious. I got the bass in and took a second to admire the pound-and-a-half monster. I thought to myself, *If you're the last bass I ever catch, at least you're a good one.*

I released the fish, gathered my fishing gear, and started the Bataan Death March home. I could hear Taps as I walked. Bo was sympathetic, but he had that better-you-than-me look on his face. We walked in silence, and when we got home, Bo disappeared as soon as we got in the house. I'm sure he went off to pray for me. But surprisingly, my mom was not upset, at least not visibly; she calmly told me to go wash up and get dressed so we could leave as soon as possible. She had laid my clothes out neatly on the bed, and as soon as I was ready, we were off.

The concert was a masterpiece for a seventh-grade or-chestra, and I played all my notes perfectly that night. But

I must admit during the entire concert, my mind was back at Bull Creek admiring the big bass that I had caught and hoping on my next trip I could catch one even bigger.

CHAPTER 4: GATUN LAKE

Panama City, Panama

One of the great things about serving in the Air Force was the opportunity to visit and spend time in some rather exotic places. Over my twenty-year career, I visited places that I either studied about in geography class or dreamed about in my dreams. One of those places was the beautiful Central American country of Panama.

The only thing I really knew about Panama was the Panama Canal. I knew the canal was an engineering marvel. It was one of the most challenging projects ever, and I couldn't wait to see it up close. It's basically a shortcut that connects the Atlantic and Pacific Oceans and significantly cuts the time for ships to go from the east coast of the United States to the west coast.

But I didn't know that when it was built, it formed a great lake called Gatun Lake. Gatun Lake is where ships wait before they enter the canal from the Atlantic side. I also didn't know the lake was full of fish, especially a bass species called peacock bass.

Major Robert Baker was my boss during my temporary duty assignment to Howard AFB, Panama. He was a big, gregarious man who had flown F-4 fighters during the Vietnam War. He was relatively quiet for a fighter pilot, and I initially thought we had little in common. But after we talked about my new job and the expectations, he asked me if I liked to fish. I lit up like a Christmas tree. Imagine that—here I was in a foreign country on a temporary duty assignment, and I met a fellow fisherman my first day on the job. I knew from that minute this was going to be a great gig, and I would have a line in the water soon.

Robert had a small boat that he liked to take out and fish in Gatun Lake. His family was not on this assignment with him, so he fished a lot and usually alone. I think he was just as excited as I was to have a fishing buddy to share this great experience. He told me all about his fishing exploits on Gatun Lake and tried to prepare me for the aggressiveness of the peacock bass. He said it felt like they would pull the boat down when they hit the line, and they never conceded to being caught even after they were in the boat. I assumed it was much like big black bass hitting the bait, but I was in for a big surprise. I listened intently to all of Robert's stories, and the more he talked, the more excited I got about getting out on Gatun Lake and catching peacock bass.

I hardly slept the night before our first fishing trip. I lived in a hotel in downtown Panama City and had about an hour drive to meet Robert at the marina on Gatun Lake. When I arrived, I was not surprised to find my new fishing buddy all packed up and ready to go. He said he rarely slept the night before he went fishing either; he was a true fisherman. At the pier, we did our preflight check—

after all he was a fighter pilot who left nothing to chance. He had thought through every detail of our trip, including alternate spots to go in case his favorite spot was slow. Bait (check), boat full of gas (check), fishing rods ready (check), ice in the coolers (check), life jackets (check), fish finder working (check), and, finally, new fishing buddy (check). All systems were go. We headed out into the lake on a warm and beautiful morning to one of his favorite fishing holes.

Gatun Lake was much larger than I thought and as deep as eighty-five feet in some areas. It wasn't long before we had our lines in the water and the fun began. I didn't have to wait long before Robert's stories became a reality. I made my first cast, and the bait sank a couple of feet in the water. Suddenly my rod was almost ripped out of my hands by what I thought was a runaway freight train. I literally had to grab and squeeze the rod with all my might to keep it in my hands, and more importantly, to keep me in the boat. Forget about reeling; I was just trying to hold on.

Robert chuckled as I struggled to get in my first peacock bass. He gave me that I-told-you-so look and offered no assistance as I worked to get the still-fighting fish in the boat. I eventually reeled in a five-pound peacock bass that was absolutely beautiful. It looked like it was built for speed and strength with the dark stripes across its lime green body and orange underbelly.

And that was just the beginning. Just as I landed my fish, Robert's drag on his rod started whining, which meant he had hooked something huge. The rod looked like it was going to break, but my new fishing buddy masterfully worked the eight-pound fish into the boat. It was obvious he had done this before because he made it look so easy. I, on the other hand, looked like I was trying to get an anchor in the boat while trying to hold on to my rod and reel at the same time.

It took catching a few fish, but I eventually got used to just how hard the peacock bass struck the line. It was such a violent tug that even when I expected it, I was still taken aback. We caught fish all day long, and once we filled the coolers, we started catching and releasing some of the fish. By the time we headed back in to the pier, I was drenched in sweat from the humidity, and my arms were aching from battling peacock bass all day. My first fishing trip on Gatun Lake was nothing short of amazing!

Robert and I fished together as often as possible during my temporary duty assignment in Panama. However, I never heard from or saw him again once I left Panama. He was not only a great boss, but he was also one of my favorite fishing buddies. One day I hope to get back to Gatun Lake and see if I can still handle those peacock bass!

CHAPTER 5: MY BIG BREAKFAST

Norfolk, Virginia

If I haven't made it clear by now, I love fishing. I love everything about it, but there is one type of fishing I just can't seem to stomach (pun intended). I had tried on several occasions, but I had never been able to enjoy the experience of deep sea fishing. The constant movement of the boat and the smell of fuel fumes from the engines spelled disaster for me. Every time I had ventured out on a deep sea fishing excursion, it has been over for me long before I got a line in the water. I was usually *sunk* by the time the boat departed the marina.

My first excursion was before I knew I suffered from seasickness. I paid handsomely to go on a deep sea fishing trip with a small crew and a few guests. I was excited about the trip and didn't give it much thought the night before. I was an experienced fisherman who knew how to handle a rod and reel as well as bait my own hook, so I figured it would be a fun trip. Everything was provided, and technically all I needed to do was show up and enjoy the experience.

I arrived on the boat dock bright-eyed, bushy-tailed, and ready to go. I had never been on a deep sea fishing excursion or a fishing boat for that matter. I boarded and chatted it up with the crew and the other guests as we were preparing to leave. I ate my usual big breakfast of bacon, eggs, grits, toast, orange juice, coffee, and a cinnamon roll—it tasted good going down.

As we pulled away from the dock, my stomach felt a little unsettled, but I figured it was due to the excitement I had for the trip. Plus, we were just getting underway. I felt pretty good as we cruised through the harbor. I watched the shoreline slowly fade into the distance.

The crew was busy doing crew stuff, and I was busy getting to know my new fishing buddies as we began the five-mile boat ride to the fishing grounds. The water was a little choppy, but the boat seemed more than capable of handling the relatively mild chop. All was going well, and I was taking in the moment of breathing the salt air while heading out to open sea. I couldn't wait to get a line in the water and pull in some of the deep sea monsters I read about on the brochure advertising the trip.

After we had been underway about thirty minutes, I began to smell the fuel fumes from the engines of the boat. The fumes made me slightly nauseous. One of the crew members noticed I looked uncomfortable and suggested I move more toward the front of the boat, so I could breathe the fresh ocean air. This felt good for a few minutes until I noticed there was no land in sight. All I could see and feel were the waves crashing into the boat.

At this point, I felt a full assault on my stomach; that big breakfast wanted out and wanted out right then. The crew member had been watching me and as soon as he sensed I was ready to throw up, he directed me to the *head* to handle my business. He knew if I didn't make it to the bathroom, he would have to clean it up.

As soon as I made it to the bathroom, I saw my breakfast again, and it didn't taste or look the same. But surprisingly, after I finished, I felt much better and headed back topside. As soon as I hit the deck, my stomach came under attack again, and now my head got into the act and started spinning like a top. I rushed back to the bathroom to get rid of more of my big breakfast and sat down to try to get my bearings. For a second, I thought everything had cleared up, but when I stood up and tried to make it back on deck, I grew weak in the knees. This time I knew I was down for the count. By the way, we were less than two hours into an eight-hour fishing trip.

My new fishing buddies and the crew avoided me like the plague. But they were all very sympathetic as they offered crackers and soda from a distance. It should be noted, no one was offering to turn that damn boat around and go back to the marina. After eight miserable hours on the roughest seas known to man (the swells were thirty feet, okay, maybe only five feet, but they felt like tsunami swells to me), we made it back to the harbor. I felt sick and was somewhat embarrassed that I never even touched a rod the entire trip. But that didn't really matter, because all I wanted was off that damn boat.

As soon as we docked, my new fishing buddies cleared a path for me as I ran toward the exit ramp. I was drenched in sweat and smelled like someone who had been throwing up for the last seven hours. There was no doubt who was going to be the first one off the boat. I literally kissed the dock. I was a little wobbly, but surprisingly I felt much better. My stomach was settled, my head had stopped spinning, and I felt somewhat normal. But I knew that was the last time I was ever going deep sea fishing.

Well, being a true fisherman, how could I not give it another shot? How can a real fisherman let one bad experience keep him from going offshore and catching one of the deep sea monsters they always talk about and catch on TV? Cancun was the scene of the crime this time, and I was in full vacation mode, i.e., do stupid stuff and hope you don't get killed while doing it. I was on vacation, and thought, *Why not give it another try?* In my defense, my friend Darryl talked me into it. I was a little leery, but after a few tequila shots, it was on, and I had fully committed to another deep sea fishing trip.

This time I was smart and didn't eat a big breakfast, and to help prevent seasickness I took a couple of Dramamine (the medicine that supposedly prevents motion sickness). There is no suspense here, and I will not build it up at all. The Dramamine didn't work—the results were the same as before—and the swells really were at least fifteen feet this time.

As I thought about it afterward, there was no way that boat should have left the harbor. Again, as soon as we got out into open water, I was down and out, and catching a fish was not an option. Just like last time, I never even got a chance to hold a rod. I found a spot on the deck and rode it out the best I could. Good thing this trip was only four hours of hell versus eight hours of double hell. I seriously considered jumping overboard just to stop the agony.

I barely survived, and my friend Darryl faked it, but he was just as sick as I was. We made it back to the marina, and I felt miserable even after I got off the boat. Darryl seemed and looked okay, but I knew better. He had stood in the same spot holding on the entire trip, and I'm sure he never touched a rod either.

We both felt like the water was just too rough on this trip and told each other that one day we would try deep sea fishing again. I had my fingers crossed behind my back and knew this was it for me. I didn't even plan to watch deep sea fishing shows on TV, because I could smell the fuel fumes through the screen. I never planned to go on another deep sea fishing trip.

CHAPTER 6: PLOOSH!!

Midwest City, Oklahoma

I was not impressed the first time I saw Draper Lake, which is located just east of Oklahoma City. The water was red, and the lake looked like a huge red mudhole. Just imagine a lake on Mars, and you have a good mental picture of what Draper looked like to me. It didn't look very promising for fishing, and with the Oklahoma wind always howling across the plains, I just didn't think fishing was going to be that great at Draper Lake. Remember what I said about fishing vs. catching in an earlier chapter; well, forget all about that. At this point in my life, it was all about catching fish.

Fortunately, I met my friend Roy Smith. Roy and I served in the Air Force together, and he was not only my friend and fishing buddy, he was my first true career mentor. Roy was older and had this very calm and patient demeanor. He is probably the most patient man I have ever known, the mark of a true fisherman. While we waited for our next bites, Roy always gave me great nuggets of wisdom on how to navigate my Air Force career and my life in general. Hindsight tells me that to Roy, it was not just about fishing.

He saw something good in me and wanted to make sure I did the best I could do in my career and in my life. Roy and I fished together as much as possible; it was our chance to get our lines in the water and forget about the worries of work. We always fished on Saturday mornings and had our traditional Southern meal of fresh fried fish and grits for lunch. Being the first customers at the local bait shop, Roy and I often had to wait for the shop to open before we could get our fishing minnows. I would get a little frustrated and impatient because this often delayed us in getting to our favorite fishing spot on Pier 19. Pier 19 was simply one of nineteen little fishing piers on Draper Lake; they keep it simple in Oklahoma.

I once thought it would be smarter to get the minnows a day early, so we wouldn't have to wait for the bait shop to open in the morning. I drove up to the bait shop and bought several dozen minnows one Friday before our usual Saturday morning fishing trip. When I told Roy, he didn't really say much, but I'm sure he knew those minnows weren't going to last through the night in my small minnow bucket.

Sure enough, the next morning as I walked into my garage, the awful smell of dead fish almost knocked me out. As Roy drove up to pick me up, I'm sure he noticed the smell, but he didn't say anything. I loaded up my gear, and we drove to the bait shop as usual to get our minnows.

On another occasion, we were fishing on a rather cool morning in early spring. We were always the early birds and usually had the pier to ourselves several hours before anyone else came. Pier 19 was about seventy feet out in the lake, and the water was ten to fifteen feet deep. We usually fished for crappie by what we called dropline fishing. We had a light weight on the line to make sure it sank and baited the hook with a minnow. We would drop the line over the railings on the pier and try to find the right depth where the fish were hanging out. Roy and I mastered this technique, and over the years caught many crappie off Pier 19.

On this particular morning, I had left my small cooler in the car and asked Roy for the car keys so I could go get it. I went to the car, and on the way back, I put the keys in my jacket pocket not realizing how shallow the pockets were. Again, it was early spring in central Oklahoma, and the water temperature was probably in the fifties. I'm sure by now that you can sense where this is going. Yes, as I got back to the pier, I forgot to give the keys back to Roy. I leaned over to check one of my lines, and, sure enough, I heard the sound, ploosh. I immediately knew what had happened, and so did Roy—the keys were in the water!

Mobile phones were not a thing then, and we were at least ten miles from home and the spare set of keys. I was in total shock and felt horrible. I immediately started taking my clothes off, thinking I could get in the water and get the keys. Roy didn't really react and kept fishing as if to say, *He'll figure it out.*

As I stripped, I began to realize that this was not the brightest idea, but I was committed to it at this point. Again, Roy didn't really react. I was now down to my skivvies, hoping Roy would talk me out of doing something stupid. Nope, he continued to fish and even came over to check one of his lines that was near where I dropped the keys in the water.

I gingerly lowered myself into the freezing water and hoped to use my feet to feel for the keys. But of course, keys dropping in ten feet of water are probably nowhere near where you think they would be. Besides there were critters in that lake other than fish, e.g., beavers, snakes, and more. By the way, I am terribly afraid of all the above.

I lowered myself into the water a couple of times before Roy finally saw the terror in my eyes, gave me the nice-try look, and helped me out of the water with this Cheshire cat grin on his face. I thought to myself, *I can't believe this great friend and mentor let me do this.* He simply said to me afterward in his calm deliberate voice, "I can't believe you did that." I'm sure there was a great life lesson in there somewhere, but to this day, I haven't figured it out, and he hasn't told me either. We eventually hitchhiked back to his house. I was red with Oklahoma mud and still shivering, but we got to his house and picked up the spare keys. You would think that would have been the end of the day. Nope, we made it back to the lake and continued fishing as if nothing had happened. As usual, we caught our fish, went home, and had fish and grits for lunch.

Roy and I are still dear friends, and we both fish as much as possible. Every time I have fish and grits, I call Roy, and we talk about our fishing trips. Of course, we talk about the time I dropped the car keys in the lake. He still hasn't told me what lesson I was supposed have learned by getting in that cold muddy water looking for those car keys.

CHAPTER 7: "SNAKE!!!!"

Edmond, Oklahoma

I am deathly afraid of snakes, and I mean any kind of snake. A twelve-inch garden snake may as well be a twenty-foot man-eating anaconda to me. My reaction is the same no matter which one I see. The following story is about an exciting adventure that involved a snake while I was tube fishing in Oklahoma.

I had never heard of tube fishing, but if it was a fishing experience that allowed me to get a line in the water, of course I was game. Tube fishing is as simple as it sounds— you have a rubber tube around your waist, wade in the water in rubber pants called waders, and cast away. As you read the following story, you will see why I only tube fished once. It was one of my best fishing days, but it was also by far one the scariest.

I met Colby Wilson while I was a youth soccer coach in Edmond, Oklahoma. Colby was a salt-of-the-earth Oklahoman who lived on a farm outside of town. After a short conversation about our kids, he asked me if I liked to fish, and we immediately had a connection. Colby began telling me about catching huge bass while tube fishing in small ponds near his house in the country. He made it seem like all the bass were huge, and as you would imagine, this got me excited about getting a line in the water. I was intrigued and happy when our conversation ended with an invite to go fishing together soon. It is worth noting here, Colby never mentioned anything about snakes.

Colby and I set a date for our fishing trip. It was spring in Oklahoma, so the weather was a little cool in the morning, a little windy, and the high temperature during the day would be in the low- to mid-eighties. We were to meet at his place early one Saturday morning to go to his favorite pond to tube fish. Colby had all the equipment, and all I needed to bring was my favorite rod with my best rubber worms.

I arrived early, and like any good fishing buddy, Colby had the truck packed and ready to go. It felt like we should have been leaving bread crumbs as we made several twists and turns on the dusty roads of the Oklahoma countryside. I was excited, but I remember thinking to myself there was no way I could find my way out of this place if something went wrong. But I could tell Colby was truly in his element; it was obvious that he had made this trip all his life and could probably do it with his eyes closed. It took us only thirty minutes to get to the pond. I was more than anxious to get started on my first tube fishing adventure.

The small pond, about half the size of a football field, was lined with thick brush and had tree limbs hanging over the water. I told Colby that it looked perfect for big bass, and he gave me a reassuring grin.

Surprisingly, it was easy for me to get into the waders and the tube, and we had lines in the water within a few minutes. It didn't take me too long to adjust to the floating sensation of the tube and to just glide through the water while casting. However, I did have a little trouble trying to control the direction of my tube, and I struggled to hit the spots where the big bass were surely lurking.

After making sure I was settled and feeling comfortable I wasn't going to tip over and drown, Colby drifted about twenty-five yards away from me. After a short while, he pulled in one of the big bass he talked about. He smiled as he held up the huge six-pounder for me to see and admire.

I was still having difficulty controlling my tube. I kept drifting into the brush and under the trees. But I did finally land a good cast in the perfect spot, right near a brush pile in a sunny spot, over a hanging limb. As soon as my worm hit the water, a huge bass jumped up and just gulped it down. The fish came so far out of the water that it hit one of the hanging tree limbs. It dragged me around in the tube until I was finally able to set the hook. The big fish jumped out of the water several more times trying to throw the hook, but he was textbook hooked, right in the corner of his mouth. All I had to do at this point was just enjoy the ride.

The fish splashed all over the place while trying to make it back to his home under the brush. But I now had full control and was just waiting for him to tire out. It took a few minutes and a lot of splashing, but I finally got the fish to my tube.

When I reached into the water to pick him up by grabbing him by the mouth, I was amazed that my entire hand fit in his mouth. It took great effort for me to get him with one hand. I knew it was a big fish, but I didn't realize how big until I started to lift him up. It felt like a dumbbell as I strained to get him out of the water.

By now, Colby had stopped fishing and had come over to help me with the monster bass I had caught. Even he seemed surprised at the size of this fish. With his mouth wide open Colby excitedly said, "He's a ten pounder if I've ever seen one." I was still trembling with excitement, but beamed as if to say, *It took a real fisherman to catch and land this big boy.* We used a stringer to tie the fish to my tube, but it never conceded to being caught and continued to splash around.

I had started casting again when I noticed in my periphery vision a small wake of waves seemed to be coming toward my tube. The wake started from the brush where I had caught the fish, and initially I just thought it was waves from the fish still splashing around. But the wake was streaking and making a beeline right at me.

Instinctively I started to back away, and just as I started to move back, Colby shouted, "SNAKE!!!" It was a water moccasin, which are known to be very aggressive, heading right at me. By then, my feet were moving like a motor trying to get me out of that water as fast as possible. Suddenly, controlling my tube was not an issue as I quickly turned and headed to the nearest shore while dragging the big fish through the water. I'm sure I was quite a sight in the rubber waders with a tube around my waist, literally running through the water to the shore.

I never did see where the snake went because once I turned around, I never looked back until I got out of the water. When I got on shore, I looked around to see where Colby was and to my surprise, he was standing right next to me. He was out of the water before I made it to shore. He was laughing out loud saying, "Man, I don't mess with no water moccasins." I told him if I had known there were snakes in that pond, I never would have got in that damn tube. He said I looked like I was walking on water as I splashed my way out of that pond.

We laughed at each other for a while before we caught our breath and began to admire the huge bass I had just caught. Colby had a fish scale in his truck, and we both guessed at the weight of the fish. He guessed ten pounds, and I jokingly said, "It has to be twenty pounds or more." I really had no clue. The fish weighed in at ten pounds and two ounces and was by far the largest bass I have ever caught before or since. Colby said he had only seen one that large in all his years fishing in the ponds near his farm. Suffice it to say that fishing trip was over, because there was no way I was getting back in that water that day or any other day for that matter.

We loaded up my trophy fish and headed home. I thought to myself, *What a great day*, but I also knew it was the last time I was ever going tube fishing.

Bill Batts and I returning from a fishing trip with two snook, Austin in the background playfully showing the size of the fish

Roy Smith holding a huge walleye caught at Draper Lake in Oklahoma City

Me holding my first big Red Fish caught at Cockroach Bay Florida

Me holding my first snook caught in Tampa Bay.

CHAPTER 8: "FISH ON"

Tampa Bay, Florida

I was not familiar with wade fishing, but was excited to see what it was like. While I was in the Air Force, I was fortunate enough to get an assignment to the Tampa Bay area; it was a great place to learn and experience the joy of wade fishing on the flats of Tampa Bay. I had no clue of how to go about getting a line in the water, but the fishing gods already had a plan for me.

It turned out my new neighbor, Bill Batts, was great at wade fishing on the flats. Just as the fishing gods planned it, Bill and I became fast friends. We were about the same age, and both had families that consisted of a wife and two young boys. Bill taught me all I needed to know about wade fishing on the flats. He even tried to teach me how to read and understand the tides, though this part didn't take too well.

Bill helped me get the right type of gear, as well as showed me the right types of lures to use for this unique type of fishing. Bill was an excellent teacher who enjoyed showing me the ropes. I think, like me, he knew he had found a new fishing buddy!

Bill and I fished in many areas of Tampa Bay, but our favorite fishing spot was an area called Cockroach Bay. Cockroach Bay is a beautiful little area with small islands of mangroves, and, like most of Tampa Bay, it was extremely shallow during low tide. Certain parts of the bay were considered no-motor zones, meaning boats with large motors were not allowed in the area. This not only helped preserve the area, but it also made cruising around the bay in a canoe a great experience.

Bill had an old Indian-style canoe that we initially just paddled around the bay. It made for some leisurely fishing, but sometimes it was just too slow in getting us to some of our favorite fishing spots in the bay. But Bill, being the engineer he was, later designed a rig for the canoe that used a small trolling motor that allowed us to cruise in and around the mangroves of the bay. We chased those redfish and snook out of their hiding places among the mangroves.

We had an absolute blast on that canoe. Bill even taught me how to set up and operate the rig, and often when he couldn't get away, I took the canoe out on my own. That was a huge step for me, and I will never forget the first time I successfully loaded the canoe on top of my jeep and headed out on a fishing trip to Cockroach Bay by myself.

The water in Cockroach Bay was so shallow at low tide that we used a rope to tie the canoe around our waist and wade fish the day away. The water could be anywhere from ankle deep to lower chest deep, but it didn't matter to us. We were wade fishing on the flats of Tampa Bay, and that's all that mattered. Initially I freaked out when something bumped against my leg, and Bill always chuckled when he saw me trying to run on water and jump back in the canoe. It felt like little sea creatures were trying to pull me under the water, but it was usually just sea grass touching my legs. This took a little getting used to, but it became a part of the adventure and fun of wade fishing on the flats with Bill. I will never forget hearing Bill excitedly shout, "Fish on," when either of us hooked a big fish. These were simply fun times with a great fishing buddy.

Bill and I fished together for the three years we were neighbors. We had some great times on the water and spent many hours just sharing life stories and childhood adventures, but we mostly talked about fishing. I say you never get to know a man until you have spent a day fishing with him, and Bill and I spent many days together. Suffice it to say, Bill and I got to know each other quite well. Though we had many things in common, our passion for fishing is what linked us. We both got the same sense of peace and calm when it came to fishing. We knew the game and played it for what it was worth; we didn't always catch fish on our trips, but it never really mattered. We had our lines in the water, and we got to share the experience with a friend and a fishing buddy!

My tour of duty in the Tampa Bay area was up, and it was time to move. It was one of the hardest moves ever because my family and I loved the Tampa Bay area. It was like being on a three-year vacation. We had family in the area, we were close to the theme parks in Orlando, we had almost year-round sunshine, and we had met great new friends. But the saddest part for me was losing my fishing buddy Bill. I had grown really close to Bill, but duty called, and I left the paradise of Tampa Bay.

Six months after we left Tampa, I got a call from Bill, and he asked me to pray for him. I was not surprised by his request because I had often shared my faith in God with Bill during our fishing trips. We generally knew where each other stood spiritually. Bill had become seriously ill, and the prognosis was not promising.

Within a few weeks, I flew back to Tampa Bay, and Bill and I loaded up the canoe and headed to Cockroach Bay. Just like old times, we chased those redfish and snook all over the bay again. I will never forget the peace and tranquility I saw on Bill's face as we fished the day away. He seemed to be in his place of comfort, the place where everything was all right, and he felt alive. Every cast seemed to have a meaning to him—it sure did to me.

I don't recall if we caught any fish that day or not, but it certainly was a great day. The day was not about catching fish, but more about the experience of fishing buddies sharing a special moment with a line in the water. You know what we talked about while we were fishing for what we both knew was probably the last time we would fish together? Fishing!

Bill passed away a few weeks later, and I went back for his final services. I briefly spoke over my old fishing buddy and wished him well on his journey to his next fishing hole. I know he will have a line in the water.

CHAPTER 9: SHIPMATE

Boca Grande, Florida

I am honored to have served in the United States Air Force for over twenty years. I was stationed at various bases all over the country and did temporary duty assignments all over the world. My favorite duty assignment by far was at the United States Central Command or USCENTCOM (CENTCOM) at MacDill AFB in Tampa, Florida. CENTCOM is a joint command where servicemembers from all branches of the military serve on one team and under one umbrella to support the Area of Operations (AOR) of Southwest Asia.

I loved everything about serving at CENTCOM—the mission was relevant and important, and the people were some of the best I served with during my military career. It was refreshing to serve with my peers in the Army, Navy, and Marine Corps, and I was impressed by the unique talents that we all brought to the table.

While I take nothing away from my peers who served in the other services, I always felt the Marine Corps officers and men were by far the cream of the crop. They had this sense of duty that I had not seen before or since. I admired these folks so much and knew deep down I didn't have what it took to serve in the Marine Corps. This has very little to do with the fishing story I am about to tell, but I felt it needed to be said all the same.

Lt. Commander George Thomas and I worked in the same office at CENTCOM. After we learned of our mutual love of fishing, we quickly became fishing buddies. I knew we were good friends once he started calling me Shipmate. I later learned this was how Navy people referred to those who served together on the same ship. After a while, we only referred to each other as Shipmate, and I don't think we ever called each other by our formal names again.

Shipmate is probably the best fishermen I ever met. He loved the water, hence the Navy, and I think he was born to fish. I love and enjoy fishing, but I think Shipmate lived to fish. He told amazing fishing stories, and not that I needed them, but he usually had pictures to back them up. MacDill AFB is located on a peninsula in Tampa Bay, and Shipmate and I often got a line in the water during our lunch break.

Shipmate had this natural knack for fishing, and when I asked him how he knew some of the things he knew about fishing, he simply shrugged, and matter-of-factly said, "I just do. I've been fishing all my life."

Shipmate and I went out on his boat and fished at various spots in Tampa Bay. His local knowledge of the area was amazing; he took me to spots that I'm sure were not on any map of the area. We never needed a fish finder because he instinctively knew where the fish were.

Shipmate and I normally caught our bait fish using a big casting net, or I should say Shipmate caught our bait fish using a big casting net. I was often an observer as he masterfully tossed the casting net off the boat and caught hundreds of bait fish after only a few casts. I was amazed at how easily he made the casting net open just before it hit the water. I could tell this was one of those things he had done all his life, and I was sure he could cast that net in his sleep.

Shipmate was eager to teach me how to cast the casting net. During one casting lesson, Shipmate carefully gathered the net, twisted the rope used to pull the net in around his wrist, and tossed it over his shoulder. He positioned himself at the front of the boat to make the cast, and just like that, he fell overboard. It happened so fast it took me a second to realize that my fishing buddy was in the water, with a casting net tied to his wrist. But before I could react, Shipmate was already at the back of the boat pulling himself onto the boat with the casting net full of bait fish. All he said was, *"That's not how you do it."* That was the end of the casting lesson for that day.

Shipmate often talked about going tarpon fishing. He wanted me to experience the thrill of catching a big "bucket mouth" before I left the area. Bucket mouth is a nickname for tarpon because of the unique shape of their mouth, which looks like a bucket. They can weigh up to two hundred and fifty pounds, and most importantly, they will fight you to the death. Shipmate told me he had never hooked a fish that fought like a tarpon. He made it point to mention that I would think differently about fishing once I hooked a big bucket mouth. Of course, this got me really excited about going tarpon fishing.

Shipmate and I set up a tarpon trip with a local fishing guide who just happened to be his brother. I thought Shipmate was the best fisherman I had ever seen until I met his brother, Captain Mike. Mike was a professional fishing guide who knew so much about fishing that I thought he had gills.

Captain Mike and Shipmate were obviously very close, and they both claimed to be the world's best fisherman. While Shipmate was out seeing the world in the Navy, Captain Mike said he was home honing his craft—he could fish rings around his big brother. Shipmate simply reminded the good captain that he was the big brother who literally put the first rod in Captain Mike's hands, and that was the end of the debate. They were both my new fishing buddies.

We met in Boca Grande, Florida, for our tarpon experience in the late spring. Boca Grande is a small town south of Tampa that is known as one of the top fishing spots for tarpon. It's not really known why tarpon congregate in this area, but suffice it to say they do.

Captain Mike had the boat ready, and we immediately headed out to Boca Grande Pass in search of my first bucket mouth. Captain Mike casually mentioned that tarpon is one of the favorite meals for sharks, but in the excitement of the trip, this comment passed right over my head. We baited up the rods with large pinfish, got our lines in the water, and began our search for tarpon.

As we waited, Captain Mike and Shipmate both told me stories of how they had fought big tarpon for almost two hours. The combat with the tarpons left their arms feeling like jello and the rest of their bodies totally exhausted from the fight. Shipmate told me I would have to experience it to really appreciate a fight with a big tarpon. I was in decent shape at the time, I worked out routinely, and I was an avid runner with good stamina. I felt like I was ready to battle a big bucket mouth. Boy, was I in for a big surprise.

After the lines were in the water for about fifteen minutes, one of the big rods started to bend and whine as the line was stretched by a big bite. Captain Mike looked at me and said, "Fish on, you're up, Shipmate. Get in the seat." The seat was a rather comfortable-looking white leather chair on the back of the boat. It had a thick seat belt, a big buckle, and a slot in the middle between the legs for the rod to be placed. The way they strapped me into the chair, you would have thought I was getting ready to drive in a NASCAR event. After Shipmate strapped me into the seat and firmly buckled the seatbelt, he said with a sly grin, "Get comfortable and enjoy the ride Shipmate. You're gonna be in this seat for a while."

I eagerly sat in the seat, thinking I would get the tarpon to the boat in short order. But the second I grabbed the rod and felt the power of the tarpon, I knew Shipmate was right. This was a different kind of fish, and I was going to be in that seat for a long ride. It was a give-and-take struggle from the start. The line would go slack, and Captain Mike would tell me to reel hard to keep the line tight. Then the fish would dive deep and stretch the line, and I could feel the seat belt tighten around my waist. It felt like I was about to be pulled out of the chair. The tarpon was not happy about being hooked and not interested in being pulled out of the water. Just when I felt like the fish was tiring and allowing me to reel him in, it got a second, third, and fourth wind and started to pull and fight even harder each time.

This went on for the first hour I fought with this fish, neither of us getting the upper hand. It seemed the best outcome would be a stalemate. Suddenly, the line went slack and Captain Mike shouted, "He's getting ready to jump." I felt a sudden burst of excitement and thought that meant I had the upper hand and had won the battle. The giant tarpon came out of the water about twenty yards from the boat. It was an amazing sight to see what looked like a five-foot, one-hundred-and-fifty-pound fish come out of the water wiggling and fighting all the way. It jumped several times, and I held onto the rod while enjoying the show and thinking the battle was almost over. Captain Mike and Shipmate both knew this was simply round one of a twelve-round championship fight, and the fish had much more fight in him. The question was how much fight I had left in me.

The battle continued as the tarpon dove, stayed deep one minute, then burst to the surface and out of the water the next. My entire body started to ache, and my arms felt weak. I was not sure how much longer I could keep up the fight. The excitement of fighting the fish had turned into sheer exhaustion, and the fish seemed to be getting stronger as I grew weaker. Shipmate and Captain Mike gave me water and wiped the sweat off my face and my head like I was a tired prize fighter. They seemed to enjoy watching me struggle with the tarpon.

I had lost track of time when Shipmate told me I had been fighting the fish for close to two hours. It finally felt like I had the upper hand, and the tarpon was letting me reel him in. It was fighting a little, but nothing like earlier. Captain Mike had just assured me that I had defeated the tarpon and all I had to do at this point was keep reeling.

I was excited anticipating seeing this huge fish up close in a few minutes. Suddenly, the line jerked violently, and it took all the little strength I had left to hold onto the rod. I stopped reeling for a few seconds to figure what had happened. When I started to reel again, it felt like the tarpon was still on, but the line seemed lighter. Just about that time we saw a huge pool of blood in the water in the area where the fish should have been.

Captain Mike shouted, "Shark." I continued to reel in the now much lighter line, and just as I saw the head of the huge bucket mouth I had been fighting with for the last two hours, the dorsal fin of a huge shark appeared out of nowhere. The shark literally ripped the tarpon off the line. It was unbelievable how fast the shark snatched what was left of the tarpon under water and disappeared beneath the surface. As I sat in the chair with the now broken line on the rod, I couldn't believe what I had just witnessed. I was too tired to be disappointed. I simply slumped over in the chair from sheer exhaustion. Captain Mike reminded me that tarpon is one of the favorite prey for sharks in the area, and when the tarpon gather in Boca Grande Pass, so do the sharks. Apparently, it was not that unusual for a shark to feed on a tired tarpon before it could be released back into the water.

We hooked a few more tarpon that day. I even got another chance in the seat and caught a decent four-foot, hundred-pound tarpon that I fought for an hour before I got him to the boat. But it was small compared to the one the shark stole off my line. Thanks to Shipmate and Captain Mike, I thoroughly enjoyed my first and only tarpon fishing experience.

After I left CENTCOM I never heard from or saw Shipmate again. But our fishing adventures, especially the tarpon fishing trip, were burned into my memory. Fishing and having a line in the water had once again been the common link that forged a great friendship.

CHAPTER 10: "DAD, DID I DO GOOD AT FISHING?"

(Edited from my first book "A Gorilla Ridin On A Half A Hot Dog")

Tampa Bay, Florida

I have loved fishing all my life and couldn't wait to take my two boys, Justin and Austin (ages ten and five), on their first fishing trip. While I caught many fish with various fishing buddies, I had also been known to spend a full day on the lake and come home empty-handed, or "skunked" in fishing vernacular. On these days, my wife would meet me at the garage door and cheerily ask, "Did you catch anything?" I would hang my head and answer, "Nope, got skunked." She never said it, but I could see that how-can-you-spend-all-day-fishing-and-not-catch-anything look on her face. Glad she never really asked, because I asked myself the same question and didn't have an answer for me either.

On the first fishing trip with Justin and Austin, I was not too concerned about them being afraid of the worms or getting hooked in the ear. My major concern was getting skunked. I thought I played it right when I had a good friend who lived on a lake who would literally feed the fish to bring them to the bank. Okay, so it wasn't exactly fishing for your next meal, but it did all but guarantee that we wouldn't be skunked.

We got all set up on the fishing dock—rods properly working, hooks on the line, bobbers set at the right depth, and worms good and wiggly. The plan was working just great. No sooner had Justin put a line in the water than his bobber sank, and he pulled up a nice sunfish; it was a wonderful moment. Meanwhile, Mr. I-can-do-it-all-by-myself Austin insisted on putting the worm on the hook himself. But he wasn't exactly sure how this was supposed to happen. I was hoping he wouldn't just decide to eat the worm; he had been known to sample dog food.

In the meantime, Justin's excitement had suddenly turned into a dilemma. I pretended to be helping Austin and didn't immediately volunteer to take his fish off the hook. I really wanted to see what my little manly man would do. The fish was flipping and flopping on the dock, and Justin seemed stuck between dropping the rod and running or just throwing the fish back in the water along with the rod and reel. I had a little chuckle, then went over to assist and gave him his first how-you-take-a-fish-off-the-hook lesson.

In the middle of this lesson, Austin who luckily had decided not to eat the worm, finally figured out how to bait his hook and got his line in the water. Like Justin, as soon as the bobber hit the water, it sank as a fish went for his worm. Now I had a dilemma, take the fish off for Justin or help Austin reel in his first fish.

Somehow, I did both. I was able to quickly get the hook released from the fish Justin had; he still wasn't too keen on touching it because it was too slimy. And before Austin's fish could pull him into the water, I was able to steady him and get him reeling the fish in. This little circle dance lasted all of thirty seconds, and afterward, the boys quickly settled into the routine of bait, cast, and catch fish. We caught over thirty fish that day, and while we took some home for dinner, we put most of them back into the lake.

The fishing trip ended up being a huge success topped off by Austin later innocently asking me, "Dad, did I do good at fishing?" I could have melted right then as I answered, "Sport, you did a great job at fishing."

CHAPTER 11: THE SAME FISH

Twin Lakes

The Hudson Valley, New York

I lived in the Hudson Valley in the small village of Monroe, New York, for over ten years. I worked in Manhattan and had an hour and half commute to and from the city every day. It was a real grind sometimes, especially during the winter, but coming home to the beauty of the Hudson Valley made it worth it. This was an interesting lifestyle for an old country boy from Georgia, but part of the beauty of life is having different experiences and making the most of them.

Growing up in the South, I experienced only two seasons, hot and humid. But living in the northeast gave me the opportunity to experience the four distinct seasons: cold snowy winters, beautiful and colorful autumns with the changing of the leaves, the burst of life during spring, and the fun and sun of summer. I loved it.

The fishing was surprisingly good in the Hudson Valley, and I found several nice lakes and ponds that made it easy for me to get a line in the water. I was always amazed at how scenic the lakes were in the area, and I would often become overwhelmed by their beauty. Sometimes the reflection of the shore and trees on the water made the ponds and lakes look like mirrors; it was breathtaking. My favorite fishing spot was called Twin Lakes, a small lake only ten minutes from my house. How convenient.

Twin Lakes had a variety of fish, including bass, crappie, sunfish, catfish, and even a few walleyes. I mostly fished for bass while using an ultralight rod and light eight-pound test line that made anything that hit my line feel like a monster fish. I routinely caught nice bass in the one-to-two-pound range, but I did catch a couple of eight pounders over the years.

The first one I caught was in the late evening in mid-summer. When I fish, and it starts to get late in the evening, I always play a game with myself and say to myself, *This is my last cast.* It's strange but I always seemed to catch a fish when I say that. Fisherman superstition I know, but it works most of the time.

I had just told myself that I was making my last cast and sure enough, just as I was about to reel my bait out of the water, a huge bass jumped out and took my rubber worm under the water. I knew this fish was huge but had no idea how huge until he jumped out of the water, and I couldn't believe my eyes. He fought like the peacock bass in Gatun Lake, diving aggressively, and jumping out of the water several times. I just knew he was going to break my rod or pop my line, but fortunately, he was well hooked, and after a few tense moments I got him to the bank. Even then it fought and jumped around, and it took a few minutes before I could handle him. It was the biggest bass I had seen since the one I caught tube fishing a few years earlier. It was the largest one I had caught in New York. Once things settled down, I was able to get a quick picture of the fish before I released him back into the water. Wow, that was an exciting few minutes, and it all happened on my last cast of the day.

A few years later, I was fishing in the same spot around the same time of year and day—midsummer and early evening. I hooked another huge bass, but this time the fish just softly hit the line and seemed to just admit defeat. The fish swam around but didn't jump out of the water and literally let me reel him in with little to no fight. My rod was bending as I reeled him to the bank. When I got the huge bass out of the water, he fought a little, but nothing like you would think a bass of that size would fight. As I looked at the fish, I just had the feeling that it was the same fish I had caught a few years earlier. Yes, he was older and less aggressive, but I was certain it was the same fish. I thought about it a second, but didn't want to keep him out of the water too long. This time I didn't even take a picture; I quickly took the hook out and put the fish back into the water. I hoped he lived a good and peaceful rest of his life in beautiful Twin Lakes.

CHAPTER 12: "GOOD NIGHT LITTLE HAROLD"

Twin Lakes
The Hudson Valley, New York

I had many fishing adventures on Twin Lakes. However, this next story is by far my favorite and most interesting. Few of my friends in New York fished so I fished alone most of the time. But that was okay, because I don't know or meet strangers when I fish. Anybody I meet while fishing is an automatic friend and potential fishing buddy.

One evening while fishing at Twin Lakes, I noticed an elderly African-American gentleman. He had set up a chair with his coffee can of worms and a cane fishing pole near one of my favorite fishing spots. He had on overalls (yes, blue jean overalls) and a straw hat, and he had a gray beard. The only thing that seemed to be missing was a corncob pipe. He reminded me of a bygone era; I had not seen anyone fishing with a cane fishing pole since I was a kid growing up in Georgia. I can't say how out of place he seemed in both area and era. I didn't notice a vehicle nearby, and I wondered how he even got to the lake. As I mentioned earlier, I fished the lake almost every day, but

I had never seen this gentleman before. I went up to him and introduced myself.

He was very cordial and spoke with a deep Southern accent. He really opened when I told him I was originally from Georgia. He told me his name was Junior B. Simpson and he was from a very small town in Georgia. I don't re-call the name of the town, but I was surprised that I hadn't heard of it because I thought I knew all the small towns in Georgia. He never mentioned where he currently lived or why he was in Monroe, New York, and I didn't press him for any information.

We talked only about fishing for an hour while he con-stantly pulled in sunfish after sunfish and placed them in a large bucket of water to keep them alive and fresh. He told me how much he loved fishing but said he never got into reels and rods and artificial bait. He always preferred his cane pole and live worms that he dug up and put in his old coffee can.

I kept casting as we talked and pulled in a few keeper bass that I offered to give him, and he gladly accepted. I put the bass in the big bucket with the sunfish, and we both laughed as they all splashed around in the bucket. I told him about myself, including my military career and my family, and how I ended up in New York. As he listened intently, he seemed genuinely proud of me. He asked me if I was an officer in the military. When I told him I retired as a lieutenant colonel, he beamed with pride and said he was happy that African-Americans were given the oppor-tunity to be officers in the military. But as we fished, I also noticed that he said little more about himself. I still didn't press him and just wanted to enjoy living in the moment with my new fishing friend.

As the sun began to set, we both looked up and simultaneously said, "What a beautiful sunset this evening." We laughed as we looked at each other. That was the first time I saw his eyes. They had a very familiar look to them—they were a little yellow with dark brown pupils. His eyes seemed to speak volumes in terms of what they may have seen in a long, hard life. We both looked away, and he quietly said he enjoyed nothing more than fishing and seeing the sunset; he only wanted to do that the rest of his life. We fished in silence the next few minutes, and I finally said it was about time for me to go. I asked him if he needed a ride home, but he said no, his daughter would be picking him up shortly.

This is when the conversation became unusual and rather interesting. My name is Harold Rickey Goff, but I am more than certain I introduced myself to Mr. Simpson as Rick Goff. As I was leaving for the night, Mr. Simpson said, "Good night, Little Harold."

I stopped in my tracks for two reasons. One, only a few folks know my name is Harold. Two, only those from the little town where I spent my early youth—Fitzgerald, Georgia—and my immediate family ever called me Harold. My mom and dad (Big Harold) are really the only people who called me "Little Harold."

I turned and asked him why he called me that; I didn't recall telling him my name was Harold nor talking about my parents calling me Little Harold. He laughed a very familiar laugh, told me that I told him all about my name, and that we talked about my growing up in Fitzgerald, Georgia. I laughed it off and thought, *Maybe I did talk about this during our conversation,* but I honestly didn't think we did.

After I left, I was driving home and thinking how strange it was that I didn't recall this part of our conversation. But I was also thinking how familiar Mr. Simpson seemed to me after I saw his eyes and heard his laugh. I even wondered more about the overalls, straw hat, and cane fishing pole. Since it was getting dark and I had left him at the lake, I decided to turn around and make sure someone did come by to pick him up. When I got back to the lake, he was gone, and I assumed his daughter had in fact come to get him. I fished at that spot on Twin Lakes for the rest of the time I lived in Monroe, but I never saw Mr. Simpson again.

I have not told anyone this story before. My father, Big Harold, was not a fisherman, and he didn't teach me how to fish. In fact, I only recall going fishing with him once, and that was after I was an adult. Big Daddy, as we called him, died a few years after I moved to New York. He and I were very close, especially the last few years of his life when I called him almost every day. While he said very little during our phone conversations, he always told me how proud he was of me. But more importantly, he told me how much he enjoyed hearing from me routinely.

I called him almost every day, but he always said I should call him "more oftener" (his words). Our phone calls often started with Big Daddy asking me, "When was the last time you went fishing?" The answer was always, "I'm on my way to the fish pond now." He knew how much I enjoyed fishing. I often told him my fishing stories, and he would laugh his deep, hearty laugh.

Over the years, I have come to think that Mr. Simpson was Big Daddy coming back to visit me. He knew where I would be, and he came back to enjoy a beautiful sunset, while we both had a line in the water.

CHAPTER 13: "SOMETIMES THEY GET AWAY"

Port Aransas, Texas

Pier fishing is one of the more relaxing types of fishing. But like most fishing, it can go from casually watching your line in the water to extreme excitement as you see your line being stretched and your rod bending over the pier. You can go from standing or sitting on the pier talking to your fishing buddy about nothing in particular and everything in general one minute to fighting something of unknown origin the next.

I had just moved to Texas, and of course, I was looking for my next favorite fishing hole. I thought it would be cool to take a trip down to the Texas coast on the Gulf of Mexico to get a line in the water. I had heard that the wade fishing was awesome, and chasing redfish again was high on my agenda. But I also wanted to check out some of the fishing piers in Port Aransas, Texas.

I planned a short day trip to the coast to do a little wade fishing. After a slow, long day in which I was totally skunked and tired, I decided to stay overnight and try my luck on the pier the next morning. One of the locals told me redfish, drum, and other types of fish were abundant around the piers, but you had to get there early because the piers often got very crowded. Early is my middle name—I was up and out well before day break the next morning.

I was the first one at the bait shop where I had to wait for them to open. I bought a few dozen live shrimp for bait and made my way to one of the local fishing piers. The pier I chose was located in a nice city park with a beautiful walkway that wound its way around the bay and into a marina. I was excited when I got to the pier and saw that it was empty. Since I was the first one there, I would get to choose the best spot.

I quickly unloaded my gear and made the long walk on the pier loaded down with my bait bucket and rods. I eventually set up in what I thought was a prime fishing spot in the far corner of the pier. It was a peaceful, tran-quil morning, and I enjoyed watching the real fishermen, e.g., dolphins and sea birds, fishing for their breakfast. The birds looked like lawn darts as they dove in the water using their beaks to spear their breakfast of little fish. The dolphins surfaced every few seconds blowing air through their blowholes as they hunted for their breakfast. I was enjoying this early morning nature show as I set up to get my first line in the water.

Just as I finished getting all my rods baited and casted, I saw three pickup trucks pull into the parking lot of the pier. I first noticed an older Hispanic man and woman get out of one of the trucks. Frankly, I was surprised at how quickly they unloaded their gear and headed for the pier. They loaded their chairs, coolers, bait, rods, and other gear on funny-looking folding carts with wheels. This allowed them to easily get everything on the pier in one trip. I thought to myself, *What a good idea,* and I knew I had to get one of those contraptions one day.

The other two trucks were full of younger adults and several of what looked like young teenage girls. While I must admit I was a little perturbed that my peaceful morning was about to end and I now had to share the pier with a bunch of teenaged girls, I was surprised that they seemed to know what they were doing. Like the older couple, they efficiently loaded their gear on the little folding carts with wheels.

As an old military operations guy, I was amazed how proficient and efficient they looked as they headed to the pier. They all looked like they were serious, and fish were about to be caught. I tucked away in the corner and continued to watch my rods for a possible bite, but I was also watching the group as they began to set up all over the pier.

In total, there were about fifteen people, and they had several rods that they expertly baited and cast in the bay. I was watching my rods when I noticed the older gentleman approaching me; he had a warm friendly smile as he reached out to shake my hand. We introduced ourselves and just like that, Arturo Gonzales and I were now officially fishing buddies.

Arturo was recently retired, and his family had decided to come to Port Aransas to celebrate. He said his entire family got up early with him to fish on the pier. After a few minutes, his wife, Gloria, also came over and joined the conversation. They told me their family enjoyed fishing, even the teenage girls, and it was a family activity they always shared together. Arturo said when he proposed to Gloria thirty-five years earlier, one of the conditions was that she had to learn how to fish. She shook her head, laughingly agreed, and said, "If learning how to fish was what I needed to do to marry the man of my dreams, so be it."

We all shared a laugh and engaged in what was a wonderful conversation about faith, family, friendship, fishing. As Arturo, Gloria, and I chatted, all the family eventually came over and introduced themselves to me. I will never forget how they all had the same warm and friendly smile of their father and grandfather. It was obvious that Arturo and Gloria were great parents, and it was reflected in the politeness and kindness of their adult children and grandkids. They welcomed me into the family as we settled in for a morning of fishing.

The fishing was slow until one of Arturo's granddaughters hooked something, and her line whined as it started to run with her bait. She was about thirteen and while she struggled a little, it was obvious she knew what she was doing. She let the line run for a few seconds and then expertly set the hook. The rest of the family cheered her on as she gained control and started to reel in her catch. She eventually reeled in a big saltwater catfish that bounced around once she got it on the pier.

Saltwater catfish are ugly, slimy, and not edible, at least I've never seen anybody keep or eat them, but they do put up a good fight. The young lady looked around to see if anyone was going to help her get the ugly fish off the hook.

But once everyone saw it was a catfish, they all pretended to ignore her and went back to looking at their own lines.

She was young and from the way she reeled in the catfish, I knew she was an experienced fisherman. But it was obvious she didn't want to have anything to do with that ugly catfish. She looked helpless as the catfish continued to bounce around on the pier before everyone started laughing.

After a few minutes one of her uncles grabbed the fish, unhooked it, and threw it back in the water. They all jokingly congratulated her for catching the first fish of the day even if it was a catfish and a non-keeper. She took the ribbing with a smile and quickly re-baited and had her line back in the water in no time. It was fun to watch them have so much fun fishing as a family.

As I watched the family, the line on one of my rods violently jerked and the rod started to bend over the pier. This was my big saltwater rod that I'd had for years but never really caught anything with it. The line was fifty-pound test line, and I always figured if anything moved or bent this rod, it would have to be something huge. I had baited the line with a very large shrimp and cast it out about thirty yards from the pier. This was the deepest part of the channel where we were fishing. I quickly grabbed the rod and jerked it several times trying to set the hook. The line suddenly went slack, and I assumed the fish had got off.

By now, the entire family had come over to my corner of the pier to watch me handle whatever was on the line. Arturo said the line went slack because the fish was running toward the pier, and I had better hold on to my rod. Just as the words came out his mouth, my big heavy rod with the fifty-pound test line almost bent over double as whatever I had hooked took the slack out of the line, and headed toward the pier.

One of Arturo's sons said it was a big redfish, while his other son suggested it was a big black drum. They were all very excited and began cheering me on to get whatever it was on the pier. The drag on the reel kept going, and I quickly began to realize I was about to run out of line. Whatever it was on the line was not tiring out and did not seem interested in being caught. I felt desperate and decided to give the line one big jerk in an attempt to turn my catch toward me and to keep it from going under the pier.

It sounded like a shotgun blast as the line snapped, and I almost fell from the recoil of the rod snapping back. A big *awww* came from Arturo and his family, as they too were excited with the anticipation of hoping to see what I had on my line. I was still trembling and a little disappointed when Arturo came over with a big bottle of water and a sandwich for me. Arturo looked at me and said in a very fatherly tone, "Sometimes you catch them, and sometimes they get away," and we toasted with our water bottles.

Some of the family members began to laugh and demonstrate what I looked like struggling with my rod and how I almost fell when the line snapped. One of the teenage girls began to give a play by play of the entire episode in Spanish, and while I didn't know what she was saying, her motions were hilarious. I felt like I was part of the family as they teased me about losing my big catch.

We caught several fish and shared many more laughs that morning on the pier. Arturo, Gloria, and I continued to share stories and the more we talked, the more cultural barriers were broken. I realized we had more in common than not. We had common family values and wanted the best for our children and grandchildren. As I packed up to leave, the entire family came over and shook my hand before I left the pier. Gloria gave me a big hug, and when Arturo shook my hand, I told him how blessed he was to have such a beautiful family. I wished him well in his retirement.

As I left the pier, I began to think to myself how once again, fishing had been a common bond that brought new people into my life. I left the pier with fifteen new fishing buddies.

CHAPTER 14: "NEVER SAY NEVER"

Sea of Cortez, Cabo San Lucas, Mexico

I ended Chapter 6 with the following statement, *I never planned to go on another deep sea fishing trip.* Well I guess it's true that one should "never say never."

I deployed to Houston with the Red Cross for a fourteen-day tour to support the Hurricane Harvey recovery effort. Without a doubt, this was one of the most humbling and rewarding experiences of my life. It will probably be another book for me one day. I worked in a couple of shelters for those affected by the hurricane and helped provide food, shelter, and other types of support. I routinely worked fifteen-hour days, but it was good, fulfilling work.

After my "tour of duty," I came home completely exhausted and slept for two days. While I was in recover mode, my friend Darryl called and asked if I wanted to go on a short golfing trip to Cabo San Lucas with him and another friend Rey, as part of my R&R (rest and recovery). I figured a little golf in Cabo would be a great mini vacation and was excited until he mentioned one little caveat—he wanted to go on another deep sea fishing trip. You may recall, Darryl had talked me into going on my last deep sea fishing trip a few years earlier. Even though he wasn't visibly as seasick as I was, I don't recall him catching a fish or even holding a rod during that trip either. We both agreed that the seas were too rough on that trip, and I thought we also agreed that we would never torture ourselves like that again.

But here he was, proposing we go on another deep sea fishing trip. Darryl had already set the trip up with a local fishing guide in Cabo. He had done the research and felt sure that the water in the Sea of Cortez would not be rough during our trip. Maybe I was just too tired to fight or just figured I could say okay and when the time came to go on the trip, I would figure out a way to get out of it. I could drink some of the local water in Cabo and really be sick!

After a few days of relaxing, it was time for our deep sea fishing trip. I hoped Darryl had forgotten or that Rey would talk us both out of it, but the trip was on. Darryl was determined to defeat the demons of the deep or go down trying. and it seemed he wanted to take me down with him.

While I didn't prepare mentally, before I left for Cabo, I purchased Dramamine tablets and a couple of motion sickness wrist bands, just in case the insanity of a deep sea fishing trip became a reality. Darryl and Rey had also gotten motion sickness medications, including motion sickness ear patches. I wasn't sure how the patches worked, but supposedly you place them behind your ears and presto, you don't get seasick.

I didn't eat much dinner the night before and no breakfast the morning of our trip to make sure my stomach was empty. I didn't want me or anyone else to see my food again. I took my Dramamine, put on my wrist bands (I only needed one, but I put one on each wrist), and strategically placed my ear patch (I thought about placing one behind each ear but decided against it) before we headed to the marina to board our boat. I looked pretty silly but figured if all the medications worked, it would be worth it.

Boarding the boat was uneventful. We met Capitan Hector and Luis, the crew of one, and headed out to sea. The boat had a nice brown leather fishing seat on the back, and as I passed it, I hoped I would get a chance to sit in it and reel in a big fish.

I immediately went up top and on the front deck to avoid smelling the fuel fumes and to make sure I could see land while we made our way to the fishing grounds. The water in the Sea of Cortez was turquoise and blue, and the waves were relatively calm. I watched the birds flying all over the place and even saw several sea lions chasing schools of fish over the water.

We made small talk as Darryl and Rey kept an eye on me, carefully watching for signs of seasickness. Since I didn't make it out of the harbor on my past deep sea fishing trips, I was pleasantly surprised after thirty minutes when I still felt great. I thought to myself, *The meds must be working.* I sensed this deep sea fishing trip was going to be different!

Luis baited the rods and got the lines out as Capitan Hector started the boat on the fishing run. It didn't take long before one of the lines on the outrigger snapped, and Luis shouted, "Fish on." Well he said something in Spanish, and I assumed it was "Fish on." While I felt fine, when

Luis called for one of us to take the seat to fight with the fish, we let Rey take it. I still wasn't so sure my stomach was ready and sensed the same for Darryl.

After the fish jumped several times, Rey landed a fifteen-pound mahi mahi (they call it a Dorado in Cabo). Darryl and I had a blast cheering him on as he fought the fish. Rey eventually got the light and dark green fish that looks sort of like a paddle board with fins to the boat. Luis gaffed the fish and pulled him into the boat while we all smiled like we had just landed Moby Dick. Good part was at least we knew we were not going to be skunked on this fishing trip.

It wasn't long before the next fish hit one of the lines and this time Darryl got in the seat to see if he could land a big one. Luis held the rod as Darryl sat down, buckled up, and adjusted into the seat. As soon as he was settled in, Luis quickly gave him the rod. Darryl began reeling, twisting, and turning in the chair trying to follow Luis's orders while Capitan Hector maneuvered to keep the fish behind the boat. Darryl began to sweat while he reeled, pulled, and finally made the fish jump out of the water. From a distance, it seemed as big as the fish Rey had caught but as he got closer to the boat, we saw that it was a little smaller. But it was big enough to go into the cooler. Darryl was excited but, of course, wished it was bigger. I was excited for him, but I also knew when the next fish hit the line, it would be my turn to get in the seat!

No sooner had the thought crossed my mind than Luis began calling for me to take my place in the seat. Another fish was on the line, and I was finally getting a chance to catch a big ocean fish. I sat down, buckled up, and Luis gave me the rod.

I immediately felt the strength of the fish as it pulled the rod and my arms toward the water. I reeled hard and tried to anticipate the next move, but I could feel the fish going deeper in the water. I instinctively began to reel and pull the rod up. The fish came up as I pulled the rod, and the giant Dorado jumped for the first time. It was beautiful, but I didn't have time to think about it because the fish was on the run again.

Luis shouted instructions in Spanish, but I just followed my instincts, and worked the rod like I had worked fishing rods all my life. After a few minutes, I got the fish next to the boat and Luis gaffed and pulled him in over the side of the boat. It was a beautiful Dorado, and he was immediately tossed in the cooler with the other keepers.

The rest of the fishing trip was fantastic; we laughed and talked, but best of all, we caught fish. At one point, Rey, Darryl, and I were all hooked up with fish at the same time. It was like watching the Keystone cops as we fought with our fish while Luis bounced from rod to rod shouting instructions to help us get the fish to the boat. Darryl and I were standing with our rods and were tossed from side to side by the motion of the boat, while Rey fought his fish from the chair. We all struggled, but eventually we all landed our fish, and then it was time to head back to the marina.

As we sailed into the marina, Capitan Hector and Luis hoisted flags on the boat with the symbols of the fish we had we caught. We had a total of eight flags with the symbol for the Dorado. We stood on the deck like heroes as all the other boat captains looked on. Overall it was a great and memorable trip. Darryl conquered his deep sea-fishing demons, and I guess in a way I did too. I finally got to experience the thrill of deep sea fishing with two dear friends that I could now also call fishing buddies.

EPILOGUE

My fishing adventures are ongoing, and I continue to meet wonderful new fishing buddies and have great fishing adventures. I continue to live in the moment when I am fishing and often laugh out loud when I slip in the water, hook myself when trying to bait my line, lose a big fish, or find myself running from a snake (ha-ha). I appreciate the fact that my childhood passion for fishing is now part of what sustains and completes me in this phase of my life. Every fishing trip is unique, adventurous, and fun in its own way. I plan to spend the rest of my life enjoying *A Line in the Water*.

ABOUT THE AUTHOR

H Rick Goff was born in the small town of Fitzgerald, Georgia. After college, he was commissioned as an officer in the United States Air Force. As a military officer, he traveled extensively and never missed a chance to smell the roses at whatever duty station he was assigned or location he visited. He is the father of two wonderful boys --now men! His first book, "A Gorilla Ridin' on a Half a Hot Dog," shared the adventures and the fun he had watching life through the eyes of his children.

H Rick Goff has run for political office, hiked trails all over the country, jumped out of a perfectly good airplane (3 times now) and spent much time with a reel and rod in his hands. His philosophy is to live life to the fullest and leave nothing on the table.